☆ SCIENCE MAGIC ☆

in the
Kitchen

☆ SCIENCE MAGIC ☆
in the
Kitchen

Richard Robinson
Illustrated by Joe Wright

Aladdin Paperbacks

New York London Toronto Sydney Singapore

*These books are dedicated to two households: firstly, the one I grew up in,
where Dad, Mum, Anne, John and Philip were forever dazzling their
gullible youngest with tricks like the ones here.
Secondly, the household I got for myself later, with Morgan and Georgia,
providing a new and demanding young audience for these same tricks.*

First Aladdin Paperbacks edition July 2001
Text copyright © 1999 by Richard Robinson
Originally published in Great Britain in 1999 by Oxford Publishing Limited
as *Science Magic: Conjuring in the Kitchen.*

Aladdin Paperbacks
An imprint of Simon & Schuster Children's Publishing Division
1230 Avenue of the Americas
New York, NY 10020

Printed and bound in the United States of America.
2 4 6 8 10 9 7 5 3 1

CIP data for this book is available from the Library of Congress.
ISBN: 0-689-84332-1

CONTENTS

INTRODUCTION

All the tricks in this book are self-working—that means you don't have to be a great magician to do them. The "magic" will be done by nature.

Magic and science have a lot in common.

Both magic and science can produce wonderful effects that leave us bewildered. Audiences always want to work out how a magic illusion works. Scientists try equally hard to understand nature's tricks.

Magicians use a lot of misdirection—getting the audience to look in one direction while the trick is being done in another; nature often seems to be doing the same. For thousands of years we thought that the sun traveled across the sky above us; now we know that the sun stays put and we do the traveling, so the Sun only seems to move. That's nature misdirecting us.

A magician's audiences will often say "I know how that's done!", when in fact they've got it completely wrong. Scientists often make the same mistake. Two thousand years ago, the Greek philosopher Aristotle had some pretty wrong ideas. For instance, he thought that apples fell from trees because they wanted to. Aristotle's ideas seem crazy nowadays, but for 1,500 years everyone thought he was hot stuff!

Aristotle's mistakes have been corrected now, but some of the magic in these books still can't be explained even by the best of today's scientists; that makes it doubly magical.

As soon as a scientist finds that an experiment has gone wrong, he or she starts again, looking and testing and guessing until he or she gets it right. As you practice these tricks you'll find that they sometimes go wrong, but with a little practice you'll get them right. Soon your tricks will seem as magical to your audience as nature seems to scientists.

Good luck.

Richard Robinson

CHAPTER ONE
COMBINING CHEMICALS

It isn't hard to find magic in the kitchen. For instance, try swallowing 250 grams of flour; follow that with a teaspoon of salt, a dollop of baking powder, two raw eggs, and 100 grams of lard.

YUK! It tastes gross.

Now, ladies and gentlemen, watch! If I mix all those things together, add some sugar, place the resulting mix in a magic box (the oven) and wave my arms for 75 minutes . . . hey presto! It's a cake. That's magic!

And shortly after that, you make it magically disappear.

Well, okay, it's not really magic, it's science that does the job. But there are a lot of similarities between a science laboratory and a kitchen: people rushing around measuring things, mixing them together, heating them, making interesting smells— and having one or two accidents!

Later we'll be looking at exactly how the stove heats things and how that can be used for some magic. We'll be using hordes of bugs as assistants in some minor miracles. We'll find half a dozen tricks to do with half a dozen eggs. We'll juggle with liquids, use levers to give you unheard-of strength—and much more.

To start with, we'll get straight down to the most scientific magic and the most magical science: **chemical reactions**. How is it that sometimes you can mix two things together and produce something different? I don't mean mixing Cocoa Puffs with milk to get a brown sludge, I mean something *completely* different!

Mix together vinegar (a liquid) and baking powder (a solid) and you get a cloud of gas bubbles. Where did the gas come from? We'll soon find out. For the moment, let's use it for our first magic trick. This one's a stunner.

THE VOLCANO ERUPTS

THE EFFECT
The magician makes a volcano erupt and pour red hot lava over the table.

YOU NEED
- Clay
- Baking soda
  (I'll call it "bicarb" from now on)
- Vinegar
- Dishwashing liquid
- Red food coloring
- A plate

SECRET PREPARATION

1 Make a volcano. Use some clay to make it in two parts: a flat base and a hollow cone for a top. Pinch the two together at the edges, making sure it's watertight and has a space in the middle about the size of an egg. Set it on the plate.

2 Mix a teaspoon of dishwashing liquid with a few drops of red food coloring. Stir this into a tablespoon of bicarb. This is your lava.

3 Drop your lava into the volcano and have the vinegar ready. Now you are prepared.

THE PERFORMANCE

1 Say to your audience,

"This is Mount Etna, the most fearsome volcano since Aunt Edna. I have the power to make it erupt at my will."

Then pour some of the vinegar into the volcano's mouth.

2 Your audience will be horrified as the volcano begins to erupt. Say to them,

"It's erupting! Run for it everyone!"

They won't need much encouraging.

WHAT HAPPENED

Mixing the vinegar and bicarb produced a fizzing foam. If you can discover what's going on amid all that fizz, you can invent some new magic tricks. And to understand the magic, you need to know a few tiny facts . . .

TINY FACTS

TINY FACT 1

You, the world, and the entire universe are made of **atoms,** like houses are made of bricks. As tiny facts go, this is about the tiniest you can get. Atoms are so small that twenty-five million millions of them would fit comfortably inside a period.

Move over! Stop shoving! Don't shove! Don't push! Give me some room!

TINY FACT 2

Atoms usually go around in bunches called **molecules**. There are only about a hundred different types of atoms, but they can be combined in millions of different molecules, just as there are only twenty-six letters of the alphabet, but they can form millions of different words.

Here is a molecule you have come across already—you created it in the last trick. It's called **carbon dioxide**, and it's made of one atom of **carbon** and two ("di-") atoms of **oxygen**.

CARBON

OXYGEN

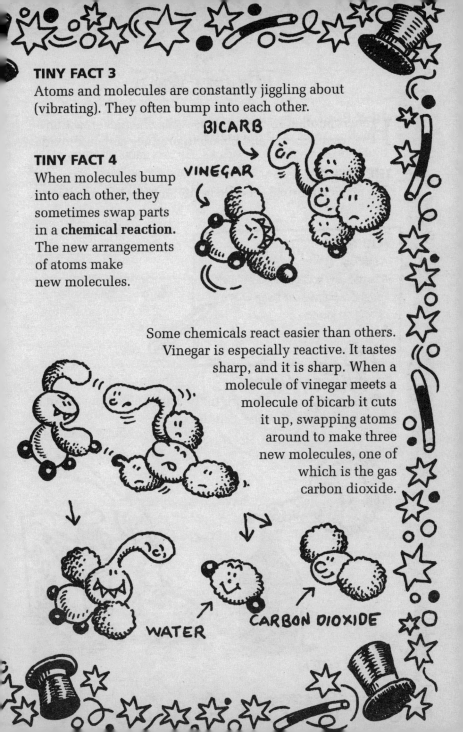

TINY FACT 3
Atoms and molecules are constantly jiggling about (vibrating). They often bump into each other.

TINY FACT 4
When molecules bump into each other, they sometimes swap parts in a **chemical reaction.** The new arrangements of atoms make new molecules.

BICARB

VINEGAR

Some chemicals react easier than others. Vinegar is especially reactive. It tastes sharp, and it is sharp. When a molecule of vinegar meets a molecule of bicarb it cuts it up, swapping atoms around to make three new molecules, one of which is the gas carbon dioxide.

WATER

CARBON DIOXIDE

BLOW UP

Here is another trick which uses the chemical reaction between vinegar and bicarb to produce carbon dioxide.

THE EFFECT
The magician brings a bottle to life! It blows up a balloon.

YOU NEED
- A balloon
- A bottle (any sort provided it's dark, so the audience can't see what's going on inside)
- Bicarb
- Vinegar

SECRET PREPARATION
Put two teaspoons of bicarb in the balloon and put about a quarter of a cup of vinegar in the bottle.

TO PERFORM

Tell the waiting world that you have the power to bring things to life. You can transmit life-giving powers with your hands. Wave your hands over the bottle in a magical way. Moan softly at the effort of beaming your energies.

Say, *"Now the bottle is alive. So alive that it wants to have a party ..."* Stretch the balloon over the neck of the bottle while you say this. *"...And it's going to blow up a party balloon to prove it."*

Add some suspense by leaving the bottle like that for 10 seconds. Nothing will happen, of course. Then say, *"Please forgive the bottle, it hasn't ever breathed before. It isn't used to blowing up balloons."*

To give the bottle encouragement, lift the balloon and jiggle it a little.

The bicarb will drop into the vinegar, the reaction will begin, the carbon dioxide will be produced, and the balloon will inflate!

Now let's find out something about that gas, carbon dioxide. Let's experiment.

THE INVISIBLE FIRE
EXTINGUISHER

Here's a trick performed 200 years ago by the "father of chemistry," Joseph Priestley, to find out more about carbon dioxide. He called it a scientific experiment, but to the folks who were watching at the time it looked like magic. It'll look like that to your audience, too.

THE EFFECT

A candle's flame is so frightened by the magician's powers that just threatening it with a soaking is enough to make it go out.

YOU NEED

- A short candle (such as a votive)
- A wineglass and mug
- Vinegar
- Bicarb

TO PERFORM

Ask a grown-up to assist you by lighting the candle and putting it into the wineglass. Pour a heaped teaspoon of bicarb into the mug and add half a cup of vinegar.
(Put a card over the glass to stop the foam from escaping.)
Explain that this flame is a very timid one. If you want it to go out, you don't need to pour liquid on it, you need only to threaten to. Remove the card and tip the foaming mug gently, as if to pour the liquid over the candle, but stop tipping just as the liquid reaches the rim. The candle will go out!

JO PRIESTLEY,
FATHER OF FIZZ

What Priestley realized was that carbon dioxide is quite heavy, as gases go. Although you can't see it, it collects in the mug just above the foam. When you tip the mug, it pours invisibly out into the wineglass, fills it up, and smothers the candle.

But you have to wonder, don't you, why Priestley was doing all these experiments. Was he just dabbling in stunts and tricks? Where was it all leading?

Well, next time a fire engine goes screaming by, remember him—many fire extinguishers use carbon dioxide to put out the flames, thanks to Priestley.

And there's one big piece of Priestley magic which you celebrate whenever you have a glass of soda, for he was the man who put the fizz into fizzy drinks by inventing a way to squeeze carbon dioxide into water. You can prove the fizz is made of carbon dioxide by getting a grown-up to hold a lighted match just above your next glassful. The flame will be smothered, just like that candle.

And that's not all that can be done with fizzy drinks . . .

A Big Tsssss About Nothing

When a can of soda gets shaken about, those bubbles can be a problem. But not if you know the secret trick . . .

THE EFFECT
A well-shaken, highly dangerous, unexploded can of soda is tamed by the magician.

YOU NEED
- Any can of soda (preferably one of your favorites, since you'll have to drink it afterward)
- Something you can tap it with

TO PERFORM
Choose a victim from the audience. Shake the can hard in front of them. Tap the can firmly five times, then open it. They'll expect an explosion. There will be a slight fizz, but nowhere near the fountain everyone expected.

WHAT HAPPENED
When you shook the can, carbon dioxide was squeezed out of the water as bubbles. These all gathered under the tab. By tapping the can, you made them all pop, so when you opened it up, instead of a fountain of foam, there was a harmless hiss.

THE OBEDIENT RAISIN

This is a bit of a puzzle for you. Work it out, then you can puzzle your audience as well.

THE EFFECT
A raisin in a glass of lemonade obeys your commands.

YOU NEED
• A glass of lemonade
• A raisin

TO PERFORM
Tell the crowd that your skills as a raisin trainer are renowned worldwide. Drop the raisin in the lemonade. It will sink. When it's nearing the bottom, say, "*Rise!*" and it will rise. When it hits the top, say, "*Sink!*" and it will sink. Keep on instructing the raisin, and it will seem to obey you.

WHAT HAPPENED
The raisin will go on and on and on going up and down: it really is very strange. Can you guess what is happening? Look closely and see if you can work it out. Turn the book upside down for a couple of clues. The answer is on page 94.

Clue 1: Raisins are heavier than water so they'll usually sink.
Clue 2: There are two things happening to the raisin: The first causes it to rise. The second thing happens at the top and makes it sink. Can you guess? The full answer is on page 94.

ACIDS

We've seen how vinegar can cut up other molecules to make new substances. "Sharp" chemicals like this are known as **acids**. Acids are as useful to scientists as a good sharp knife is to a chef.

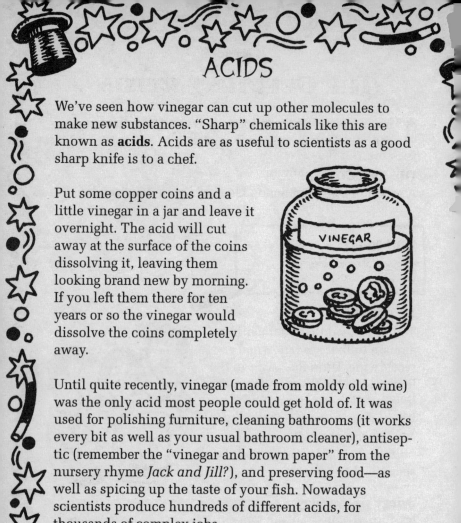

Put some copper coins and a little vinegar in a jar and leave it overnight. The acid will cut away at the surface of the coins dissolving it, leaving them looking brand new by morning. If you left them there for ten years or so the vinegar would dissolve the coins completely away.

Until quite recently, vinegar (made from moldy old wine) was the only acid most people could get hold of. It was used for polishing furniture, cleaning bathrooms (it works every bit as well as your usual bathroom cleaner), antiseptic (remember the "vinegar and brown paper" from the nursery rhyme *Jack and Jill?*), and preserving food—as well as spicing up the taste of your fish. Nowadays scientists produce hundreds of different acids, for thousands of complex jobs.

But acids can also be dangerous, as dangerous as a knife in the hands of a baby. Power stations pump out sulphur dioxide as they burn coal. This dissolves in the atmosphere and falls as acid rain, eating away at buildings and polluting lakes. Swedish scientists pour lime into their lakes to try and combat the effects of acid rain. Lime is an **alkali** . . .

ALKALIS

Alkalis are another group of "sharp" chemicals. Acids and alkalis can both be energetic reactors, but they work in opposite ways. Put them together and they will cancel each other out (**neutralize** each other). For instance, a wasp sting is alkali, so putting vinegar (acid) on it will neutralize it and make it feel better. But a bee sting is acid, so you need an alkali like bicarb to make it feel better. Remember:

BICARB FOR A BEE
VINEGAR FOR A VASP

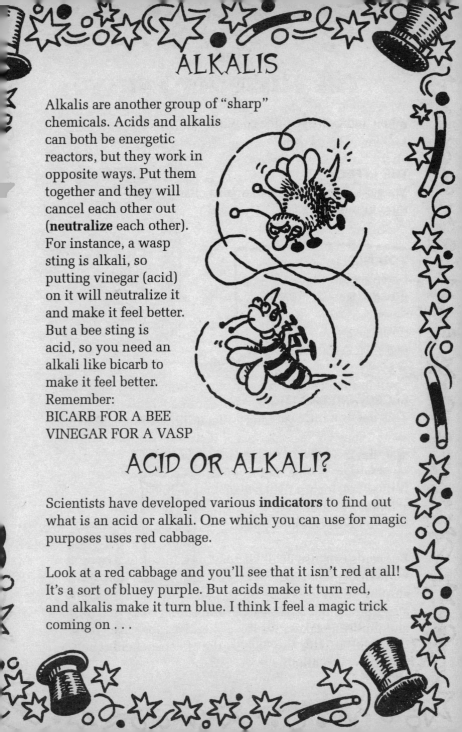

ACID OR ALKALI?

Scientists have developed various **indicators** to find out what is an acid or alkali. One which you can use for magic purposes uses red cabbage.

Look at a red cabbage and you'll see that it isn't red at all! It's a sort of bluey purple. But acids make it turn red, and alkalis make it turn blue. I think I feel a magic trick coming on . . .

THE FUSSPOTS' PARTY

See red cabbage juice go wild!

THE EFFECT
Your magic powers make drinks change color
miraculously.

YOU NEED
- Three glasses
- Red cabbage
- Bicarb
- White vinegar
- Hot water in a bowl
- A sieve

SECRET PREPARATION
This needs a little care in setting it up, but it's worth it.

1 Put a teaspoon of bicarb (an
alkali) in the first glass, then
fill to near the top with water.
When it has dissolved it
should look colorless.

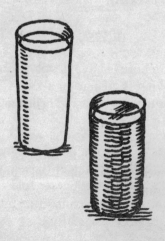

2 Get a grown-up to chop a
big handful of slivers off the
red cabbage. Soak them in hot
water for about 5 minutes. You
should then have a purple
liquid. Strain this through a
sieve into the second glass.

3 Fill the third glass with vinegar. It should look colorless.

TO PERFORM

To begin with, keep the glasses out of sight. Just start the patter like this . . .
"Once upon a time, the Emperor Julius Caesar invited his friends Brutus and Antony over for tea.'Let's have a drink,' said Caesar. 'Here's some water for you, Brutus ...'
(produce glass 1 and place it to the left)
' ...and here's some water for you, Antony ...'
(produce glass 3 and place it to the right) *'... and here's some grape juice for me ...'*
(produce glass 2, the purple one, and place it in the middle).

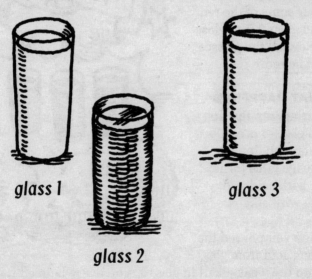

glass 1

glass 2

glass 3

Brutus said,'Oh! Why have you got grape juice while we have to make do with water? I don't want water! I want blueberry juice!' Caesar said, 'Then you shall have some.' (Pour some of the purple juice into glass 1. The "water" will turn blue magically.)

Antony said, 'I don't want water, either! I want strawberry juice.'
'Then you shall have some,' said Caesar.
(Pour some of the purple juice into glass 3.
This "water" will turn red.)

Brutus said, 'Actually, I would rather have strawberry juice as well.' Caesar said, 'No problem.'
(Pour some of the red from glass 3 into glass 1. It will turn red, too.)

'In fact,' said Caesar, 'I think I'd prefer strawberry juice, too.'"
(Pour some of the red from glass 3 into glass 2. Now all the glasses will be red.)

WHAT HAPPENED
Pouring into the first two glasses is easily explained: Red cabbage juice turns red with acid and blue with alkalis.

When you poured the strong acid from glass 3 into the weak alkali in glass 1, you overwhelmed it. So the solution became mostly acid and turned red. The same happened with the strong acid and the indicator in glass 3.

When you've practiced this trick a few times to get the mixes right, it will be a dazzler.

LAZY POLISH

This alkaline chemical reaction is for getting into your family's good books if they have any silver ornaments. Silver gets dirty very easily and if it's kept in sunlight it turns black. People can spend a long time with rags and polish and hard rubbing to get the silver bright again.

THE EFFECT
Get dirty silver clean with no effort at all.

YOU NEED
- A bowl of warm water
- Dirty silver
- Aluminum foil
- Baking powder

TO PERFORM
Dissolve a teaspoon of baking powder in a bowl of warm water. Wrap the silver loosely in the foil and put it under the water. Now leave it for a day. That's all. The silver will be magically clean, with no effort.

WHAT HAPPENED
The tarnish on the silver was caused when it reacted with chemicals in the air to form a new, dull-colored substance. The bicarb reacted with the tarnish to reverse this process, restoring the silver to its original purity.

MAKING OXYGEN

Jo Priestley (see page 17) was especially excited to discover what this awesome gas, oxygen, can do. It's one of the most dangerous gases because it makes our houses burn down and rusts metal. And it's one of the most useful, because we breathe it to give us energy. Factories churn out great galloping amounts of the stuff in cylinders and tanks for use in everything from oxy-acetylene welders to rocket engines. Why don't you set up your own factory?

THE EFFECT
The magician makes a stick burst into flame.

YOU NEED
- Liver from the butcher
- Hydrogen peroxide from the pharmacy
- A wood splint, such as a kebab stick

TO PERFORM
Pour some hydrogen peroxide on the liver and there will be a furious reaction. Get a grown-up to assist you by lighting the wood splint. Then tell them to blow it out and put the red-hot tip in amongst the bubbles. The splint will burst into flame with a little pop.

WHAT HAPPENED
The gas produced is oxygen. Oxygen is needed for things to burn, so when the red-hot tip is put into the bubbles, it reignites itself.

MAGIC CHANGES
IN YOUR BODY

So, what do we know? Mixing the right things up in the right way can make them all change their nature in a chemical reaction. That's what happens in your body, too. You put the right things in your mouth (and according to your parents, lots of wrong things), and all the acids and juices inside you change them miraculously into muscle, bone, hair, brain (sometimes), spots, toenails, and energy.

Usually the chemical processes are locked up inside you. You get a hint of what's going on when you are sick. The body has decided that you've definitely put the wrong stuff inside you, and shoves it out again. That sharp taste in your vomit is acid from your stomach, which has been busy slicing your food up, dissolving it for use around your body.

You can get a hint of the digestion process without having to make yourself sick, because a small part of it starts in your mouth. You can use this knowledge in a little bit of magic.

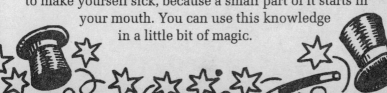

CHANGING SALT INTO SUGAR

YOU NEED
- A small teaspoon of salt
- A teaspoon of flour
- A plate

TO PERFORM

This is a one-to-one trick. Put a tiny pinch of salt on the plate. Ask someone to taste it to prove it is genuinely salt. Tell them that you can change salt into sugar just by adding flour.

Mix the flour with the salt. Ask them to put some of the mix on their tongue and wait for a few seconds. They will taste sugar!

WHAT HAPPENED

Your assistant thinks you've turned salt into sugar, but actually it's the flour that has been changed. The saliva in the mouth does it as it begins the digestive process, breaking down the flour into sugar ready to be used by the body. The salt merely speeds up the change so it's noticed quicker!

CHAPTER TWO

Heating Up

Why do cooks cook? What is heat? How come humans had to invent cooking before they started on wheels, windmills, sweaters and washing machines? Before we can come to grips with this, we need one more tiny fact.

TINY FACT 5

When atoms and molecules get hotter, they move faster. When these hot, fast moving molecules barge into your skin, you feel it as heat. So, heat is movement, right? Let's prove it. Rub your hands together. Do they feel hot? That's because you've made all the skin molecules move a bit faster. If you rub two sticks together, the wood gets hotter and the molecules move faster and faster until they are barging into each other so hard that they start cracking up into atoms. The atoms crash around and recombine. So now instead of molecules of wood, we have molecules of carbon dioxide, carbon monoxide, water, and carbon, plus heat and light. We call this a fire!

When scientists want chemicals to do things faster, or cooks want to turn ingredients into food, they use heat.

MAKING PLASTICS

Plastics are the wonder of our age. Strange to say, scientists make plastic from perhaps the most gruesome muck you could imagine—plants that died two hundred million years ago and have been rotting underground ever since. This foul, stinking brew is called oil.

The chemical magic that turns oil into a Barbie doll is complex and clever. Luckily, you can do something similar on the stove in your kitchen without having to drill for oil in the backyard.

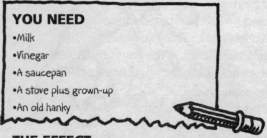

YOU NEED
- Milk
- Vinegar
- A saucepan
- A stove plus grown-up
- An old hanky

THE EFFECT
The magician turns milk into plastic.

TO PERFORM
Get the grown-up to warm a cupful of milk, then add a quarter of a cupful of vinegar. The mixture will separate into a thick white material—plastic—and a more watery solution.

Pour it through the hanky, then wash under cold water and strain and squeeze it to get the plastic into a ball. Within 2 hours it will dry rock solid.

Without heating the milk, the reaction wouldn't happen.

THE HEAT GOES ON

How does the heat get from the stove to the saucepan to the middle of the milk?

Imagine you are a saucepan molecule. Let's say you're that one just there, seventy-three millionth from the left in the nine billion and forty-third row. What happens if a mass of violently jiggling hot oven molecules comes charging toward you? As they knock into you, they make you jiggle too. And your neighbors. Pretty soon you are jiggling as hard as the oven molecules. In other words, you are all the same temperature.

Of course, now that you're boogying away, you knock into the molecules behind you, and they start on the ones behind them. The heat is being moved through the saucepan, and from there through the food, until you are all cooking away together. This is called **conduction.**

I'm a good conductor too!

Some things conduct heat faster than others. Look around. Some kitchen things have wood or plastic handles. These don't pass the jiggling on so well, so they warm up more slowly. They are bad conductors. Saucepans are made of a good conductor, metal, which transmits heat very fast.

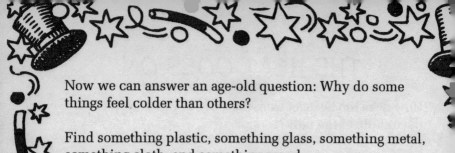

Now we can answer an age-old question: Why do some things feel colder than others?

Find something plastic, something glass, something metal, something cloth, and something wood.

You may think that if they've been in the same room for a while they should all be the same temperature. But if you touch them, some feel cooler then others.

You are warmer than the other things in the room. So when you touch a good conductor it whisks your heat quickly away, and at the surface it remains cooler than you. When you touch a bad conductor, it keeps your heat right there at the surface, so it feels the same temperature as you.

The next trick is based on heat conduction.

COOL SPOONS

THE EFFECT
The magician can tell which of three spoons has been chosen by a member of the audience, simply by touching them.

YOU NEED
- Three metal teaspoons
  (it's best if you leave them in the fridge
  for a few minutes before the trick)
- A blindfold (a pillowcase over the head is good)

TO PERFORM
Lay the spoons out in a row and put on the blindfold. Ask someone to pick one up. Tell them you are going to tell which spoon they've chosen by reading their mind. Ask them to press it against their forehead with the palm of their hand for 20 seconds or so, to help transmit the mental waves, then put it down.

Pick up each spoon in turn, secretly feeling the temperature, and saying, *"Now was it this one ...or this one ...or this one? I think it was this one!"* Hold up the warmest spoon. They'll be amazed.

WHAT HAPPENED
While they hold the spoon in their hand, their body heat is conducted into the metal, so the spoon gets warmer.

KITCHEN HINTS—1

Use your knowledge of conduction to make life in the kitchen easier.

A TOUCH OF GLASS
Glasses can crack if you pour very hot water into them—not any more! Put a metal spoon in the glass when you pour. The metal conducts the heat away from the glass so fast that its temperature is kept below the cracking point.

A HALF-BAKED IDEA
Baked potatoes always seem like a simple meal to have, but why do they take forever to cook in a conventional oven?

A potato is a bad conductor of heat. It takes ages for the heat to get to the middle of the spud. So push a metal fork or skewer into each one. Now the heat will be conducted along the metal right to the center of the spud. Magically cuts cooking time in half!

MAKING THINGS BIGGER

Heating things makes them bigger. The warmer something is, the bigger it gets. How so?

All right, so you're a molecule once more, surrounded by millions of your friends. You're all cool molecules, so you're just hanging loose, jiving gently. What happens when you're made hot? Suddenly you find yourself jiving harder. Naturally you bump into your neighbor, who moves away and bumps into their neighbor. Let's face it, you need more room to dance. The whole crowd of you needs to take up more space, or **expand.**

If you don't believe that, do this. Put a big jar into a saucepan on the stove. Pour water into the jar until it's brimming. Pour a cupful into the pan. Get a grown-up to put the stove on, and watch. As the jar heats up you will see water begin to trickle down the side, forced out by the expanding water below.

You may have heard of the "greenhouse effect." Scientists believe that the whole Earth is warming up steadily. You can imagine what is happening to all the water in the oceans: it's expanding, so sea levels are rising. Some islands in the Pacific are only a couple of feet above sea level at their highest point. They are likely to disappear completely over the next few years.

KITCHEN HINTS—2

OPEN SESAME!
OPEN MARMALADE!

Be patient. One day soon, someone near you will be unable to get a metal lid off a jar. You can help them with your magic powers. Tell them to pour hot water from the sink over the lid but not the jar. After a few seconds the lid will unscrew easily! (The metal lid expanded and became bigger with the heat—not a lot, but enough to loosen its grip on the jar.)

PING-PONG POPPER

Be even more patient; some time in the next ten years you will be the proud owner of a dented ping-pong ball. Do not despair, you will know what to do. Get a grown-up to put it in a kettle of water, then boil it. In a few seconds the dent will pop out. In this case its the air inside the ping-pong ball expands and pushes the dent out.

THE TALKING BOTTLE

*G*ases expand farther than solids, that's why this next trick works so well.

THE EFFECT
The magician makes a bottle talk.

YOU NEED
- A coin
- An empty wine bottle

SECRET PREPARATION
The wine bottle must be very cold, so leave it in a freezer for half an hour before the trick.

TO PERFORM
Place the freezing bottle on the table, telling everyone that it's a very chatty bottle—although it's a bit shy and might not talk if it knows there are people in the room. Ask everyone to be very quiet.

Wet the top of the bottle and place the coin on it, nice and straight, with no air gaps. Place your hands on it. Keep absolutely still and concentrate on making the bottle speak. (Your hands are doing the magic. They are warming up the glass, which is warming up the air, which is expanding . . .)

The bottle starts to speak! It talks in clicks (well, you wouldn't expect rhyming couplets—it is only a bottle, after all).

WHAT HAPPENED

The clicks are caused by the expanding air forcing its way out by pushing past the coin. The coin drops down with a click before being lifted by the next blip of air.

CHAPTER THREE

MAKING THINGS SMALLER

If heating things makes them expand, then cooling them should do the opposite—make them become smaller, or **contract**. There's some more magic to be found here.

✳ Magic ✳

THE TIME BOMB

THE EFFECT
The magician makes a plastic bottle self-destruct.

YOU NEED
- A plastic soda bottle
- A hair dryer

TO PERFORM
Place the top on the bottle, but don't screw it on—yet. Give the bottle a good blast with the hair dryer for about 20 seconds to warm up the air inside, then screw the top on really tight and wait. In a few seconds' time the bottle will suddenly collapse.

WHAT HAPPENED
As you warmed up the air it expanded, squeezing some out of the top. When you screwed the top closed, you shut in fewer molecules than had been there before. As they cooled, they took up less space, the air contracted.

UNDER PRESSURE

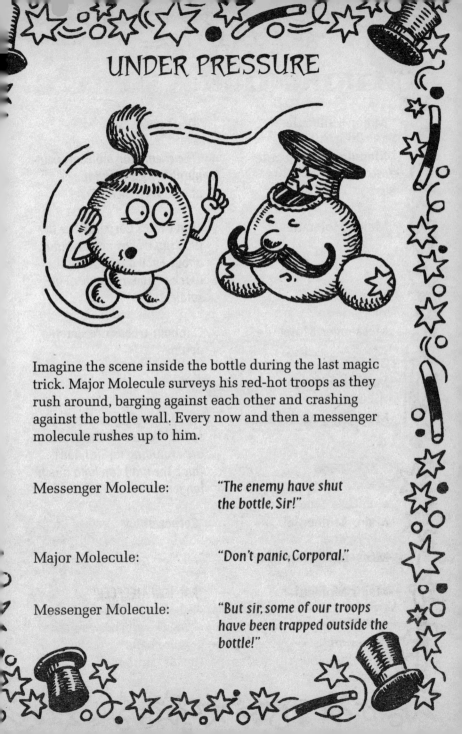

Imagine the scene inside the bottle during the last magic trick. Major Molecule surveys his red-hot troops as they rush around, barging against each other and crashing against the bottle wall. Every now and then a messenger molecule rushes up to him.

Messenger Molecule: *"The enemy have shut the bottle, Sir!"*

Major Molecule: *"Don't panic, Corporal."*

Messenger Molecule: *"But sir, some of our troops have been trapped outside the bottle!"*

Major Molecule:	"Don't panic, Corporal."
Messenger Molecule:	"The enemy air molecules outnumber us, Sir. Will we be able to keep them back?"
Major Molecule:	"Have faith, Corporal. See the way my troops are rushing about. Each one is doing the work of two molecules. Fine soldiers!"
Messenger Molecule:	"Sir, your troops are slowing down."
Major Molecule:	"What!"
Messenger Molecule:	"They're cooling and losing speed. The outside molecules are crowding in, Sir. I don't think the wall can hold much longer."
Major Molecule:	"Corporal?"
Messenger Molecule:	"Sir?"
Major Molecule:	"PANIC!!! AIEEEEE!!!"

Air molecules are a pretty irresistible force. They crowd out the atmosphere in vast numbers, towering up 80 km to the edge of space. So you have a column of air 80 km high sitting on your head, as heavy as 80 bags of sugar. You don't notice this, because you're used to it; you've been coping with it all your life. But that **air pressure** is your secret weapon in the next piece of magic.

We can remove a little of the air in a closed container by burning some paper in it. When things burn, they use oxygen, which is about a fifth of the air. So that should allow us to see the power of the atmosphere pretty well in the next two tricks.

80 KM

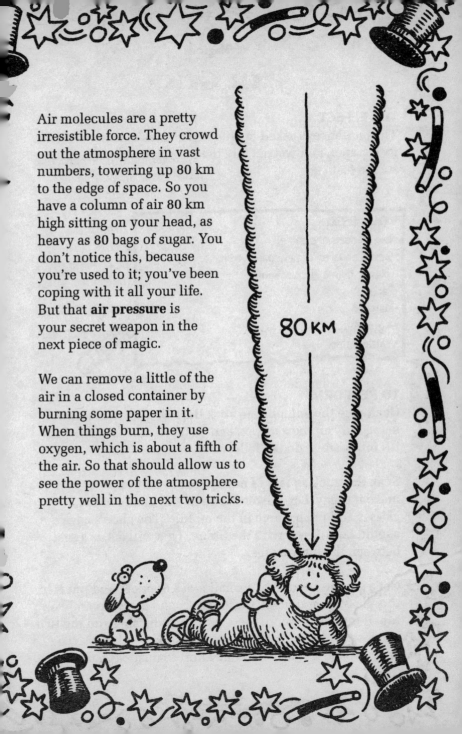

AIR GLUE

THE EFFECT
The audience is asked to glue two glasses together with air, newspaper, and water. Only the magician can accomplish such a feat.

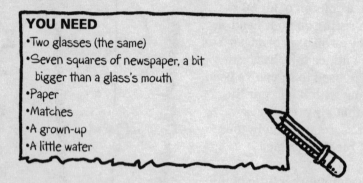

YOU NEED
- Two glasses (the same)
- Seven squares of newspaper, a bit bigger than a glass's mouth
- Paper
- Matches
- A grown-up
- A little water

TO PERFORM
Challenge the audience to stick the two glasses together using only air, newspaper, and water. When they tell you it's impossible, do the following:

Soak the thick square of newspaper in a little water to make it soggy. Lay it over the open end of one of the glasses and poke a hole in the middle. The glass's edge should be covered with the tissue. This will act as a seal between the two glasses.

Get a grown-up to light a small piece of paper and put it in this glass, then quickly place the second glass squarely on top. If the seal is good, there will be no hissing and the two glasses will be stuck together—that's the good news. The bad news is, it'll take a titanic effort to unstick them.

WHAT HAPPENED

On page 40 the plastic bottle was crushed by the weight of the atmosphere as the air inside contracted. In this case the glasses don't buckle, but the atmosphere still presses in. It is this which keeps the two glasses together.

THE MAGDEBURG SPHERE

In 1654, this same demonstration was performed in the small German town of Magdeburg, with quite extraordinary results.

Otto Von Guericke had just invented a rather neat air pump. For his own amusement he thought of something wacky to do with it. He decided to pump all the air out of a can, so that he had . . . well, so that he had a can of nothing at all—what we call a **vacuum**. But it wasn't so easy. Whenever he got halfway through the pumping, his cans would collapse. He began to realize the enormous power of the atmosphere pushing in on his vacuums.

Otto devised a piece of Very Big Magic of his own. He had two half-spheres, about 40 cm across, built out of thick bronze. "These won't collapse in a hurry," he thought. Placing them together snugly, he rigged up his pump and

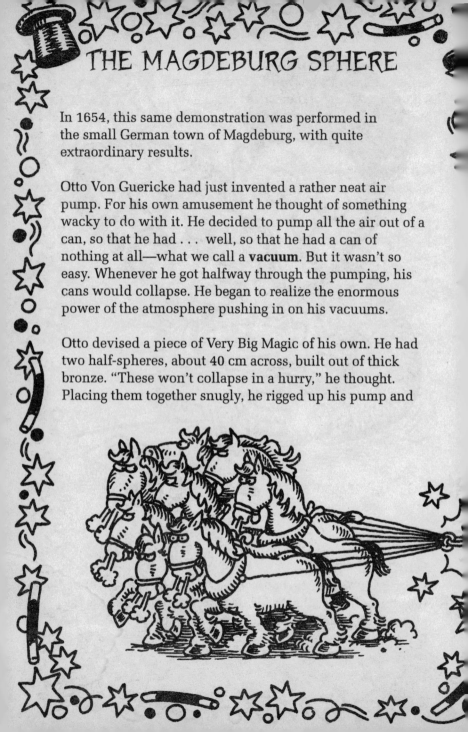

pumped away until there was nothing left inside. (This was the world's first vacuum.) Then he tried to get them apart . . . and he tried . . . and tried . . . and tried.

Eventually he had to employ sixteen horses to heave the sphere open, such was the power of the atmosphere pushing in on his bronze ball.

Why should a teapot remind you of Magdeburg? Next time you are near a teapot, look at the lid. You'll see it has a hole in it. What would happen if the hole wasn't there? As the air inside the pot cools, it contracts. Without the hole, the lid would be pressed into the pot by atmospheric pressure. You'd need Otto's horses to get it off!

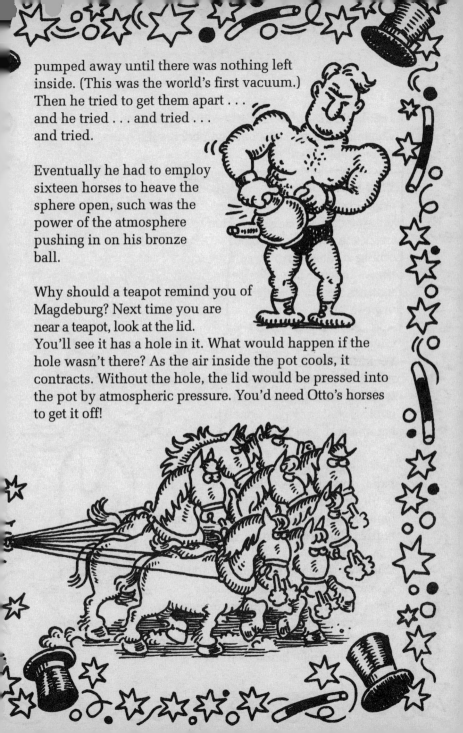

BANANA PEELER

THE EFFECT
The magician makes a banana peel itself.

YOU NEED
- A glass bottle
- A banana (pick one the same thickness, when it's peeled, as the neck of the bottle)
- Paper
- Matches
- A grown-up

TO PERFORM
Ask the audience if they can peel a banana without touching it. When they confess that they can't, take the banana and peel back the very tip.

Ask the grown-up to light a little of the paper and put it—still flaming—into the bottle. Quickly insert the tip of the banana, leaving the skin outside the bottle. Make sure there are no air holes.

While you watch, the banana will be squeezed into the bottle, pushed into it by atmospheric pressure outside as the oxygen inside is used up. (Don't plan on eating the banana—it will be covered with soot and burnt paper. You'd have to be bananas to try!)

There's A Sucker Born Every Minute

THE EFFECT
In a race to drink a glass of juice, the magician wins every time.

YOU NEED
- Two drinks
- Two straws
- One pin

SECRET PREPARATION
Make a large pinhole about 3 cm down each straw. The holes should be big enough to fit a matchstick.

TO PERFORM
Challenge someone to a drinking race. Give them a drink and a straw, and off you go. But make sure as you drink, you are holding your straw with your thumb covering up the hole. That way, your drink will be sucked up in the usual fashion while your opponent will get nowhere.

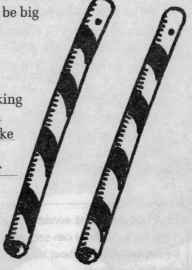

When you are halfway through your drink, notice your opponent is having difficulties and offer to swap drinks. Perhaps they'll think your straw has nothing wrong with it. But they'll be disappointed. They'll still find it impossible, while you can secretly cover their straw's hole and finish off their drink.

WHAT HAPPENED

When you suck, you remove some of the air from the top of the straw. Atmospheric pressure at the other end forces some liquid up to fill the gap. If there's a hole in the straw, then air can leak straight through it, and the drink is untouched. So your secret stooge in this trick is the entire atmosphere, and nobody can spot it!

Practice note: ___ f the trick lies in being able to handle the straw so that no___ ou covering the hole. When you practice, ___ manipulating ___ king. With tricks like this, it's the eyes that

CHAPTER FOUR
SOLIDS, LIQUIDS, GASES

So when things warm up they expand and when they cool down they contract. When they warm or cool a lot, interesting things happen. Take water, for instance. Look what happens to the molecules . . . oh, you can't. They're too small. The best way to see one is to *be* one.

Look deep into my eyes ...you are feeling very small ... ve-e-e-e-ry small....You are no bigger than a molecule of water.... Those things whipping around your head are your fellow molecules. Now fasten your seatbelt; you're in for a busy day. First we'll cool you down—all of you. You are feeling sleepy....You want to speed around a lot less ...and less. You are coming closer together, you are contracting....Now you're so close you can link arms. You have become a solid—ice!

You might be stuck to the side of a freezer, floating in someone's drink, hanging off a drain spout inside an icicle, floating through the air as a snowflake, aiming at someone's neck, packed into a snowball—

OK, enough of that! Now let's get you all jiving again with a bit of heat....Faster! ...Faster! Now you're a liquid again, you and the rest, swinging around each other like a huge demented country dance. Now you're being heated more. The dancing's getting wilder. No time to dosey-do, you're all flying off every which way. You have become a gas—steam!

You might be flying out of a kettle spout, pushing a piston in a steam engine, or taking part in the climax of the next piece of magic . . .

POPCORN

Popcorn is very easy to cook. Ask a grown-up to help you do it. All you need is a saucepan with some oil and a handful of popping corn.

But what happens when the corn pops? Inside each of those hard kernels is a little water—not a lot, but enough. When the corn is heated, the water turns to steam, which is a gas and needs more space. The only way to find space is to break out of the kernel—to explode it like a small grenade.

That's how popcorn pops. It's also the key to the steam engine and the Industrial Revolution.

✳ Magic ✳

HERO'S HEROIC EFFORT

In its prime, 100 years ago, the steam engine powered the world. Trains, boats, factories, and mines all depended on it. Even now, it powers the generators which make electricity—and all because of the incredible way water expands when it turns to steam.

You can experience this by making the earliest steam engine, the one created by the famous inventor, Hero of Alexander, 2,000 years ago.

WHAT TO DO

Make a large pinhole on either side of the can, near the top. (Careful, use the technique on page 18 or it will spray all over you.) Let the soda trickle into a glass, but leave a few centimeters in the bottom of the can. Bend the two holes with a pin until they both point around the tin in the same direction. You can string the thread under the tab on top.

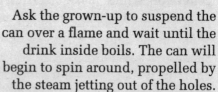

Ask the grown-up to suspend the can over a flame and wait until the drink inside boils. The can will begin to spin around, propelled by the steam jetting out of the holes.

With the rest of the can's contents, drink a toast to Hero of Alexandria.

SO WHAT WAS WATT?

We usually say the steam engine was invented about
200 years ago by James Watt. As you see with Hero's
invention, the idea had been around for at least 1,800 years
before that. But in all that time, it was never more than
an interesting toy.

By 1700, there was a need for something more practical. In
particular, mines needed to be pumped free of leaking water,
and the engines they had were not too good at doing that. In
1705 Thomas Newcomen invented a steam engine which
relied on the kind of effect you used in the Air Glue trick.
Steam was jetted into a cylinder, forcing a piston through it.
Then the whole cylinder was doused with cold water, the
steam contracted as it cooled (**condensed**), and the piston
was pushed back down again by atmospheric pressure.
Newcomen's engine was called the "atmospheric steam
engine." It was good—but it wasn't great.

From 1769 onward, the brilliant mind of James Watt created a stream of improvements to the basic engine. One of the first things that struck him was that it was a waste of time heating up the piston cylinder with steam if seconds later you were going to cool it down again with water. So he simply put the cooling unit in another place. The "separate condenser" tripled the power of steam engines at a stroke. He also reckoned that if you were going to pump steam in at one end to push the piston up, you may as well pump it in the other end to push the piston down again. He also introduced the idea of lubrication with oil, he added gears, a throttle, and automatic control systems. . . . The list is a long one.

So although Watt didn't actually invent the steam engine, his name is rightly honored to this day—although in a rather odd way. Next time you buy a 60-watt light bulb, remember: Those watts are James Watt's watts!

SOLIDS AND
LIQUIDS—THEY'RE A GAS!

In your everyday dealings with the planet, you depend on things being reliably liquid, solid or gassy. For instance, you wouldn't ride on a bus if you thought it would turn to liquid any second. You wouldn't bite into a sandwich if it was about to turn to vapor.

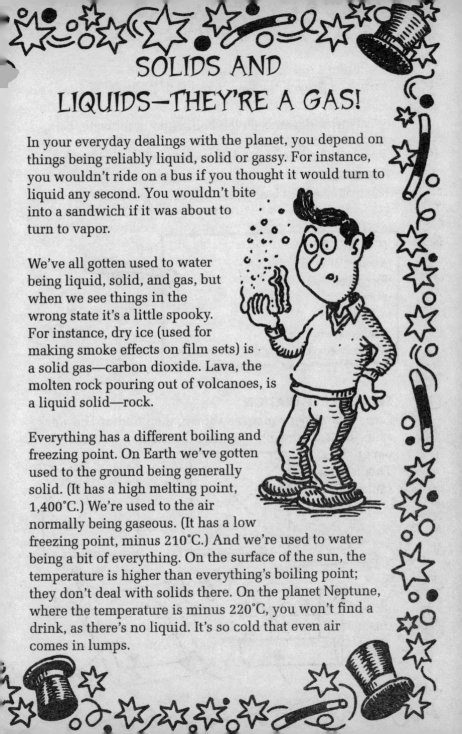

We've all gotten used to water being liquid, solid, and gas, but when we see things in the wrong state it's a little spooky. For instance, dry ice (used for making smoke effects on film sets) is a solid gas—carbon dioxide. Lava, the molten rock pouring out of volcanoes, is a liquid solid—rock.

Everything has a different boiling and freezing point. On Earth we've gotten used to the ground being generally solid. (It has a high melting point, 1,400°C.) We're used to the air normally being gaseous. (It has a low freezing point, minus 210°C.) And we're used to water being a bit of everything. On the surface of the sun, the temperature is higher than everything's boiling point; they don't deal with solids there. On the planet Neptune, where the temperature is minus 220°C, you won't find a drink, as there's no liquid. It's so cold that even air comes in lumps.

PAPER SAUCEPAN

This trick depends on the boiling point for water being 100°C. Luckily, it is.

THE EFFECT
The magician can boil water in a saucepan made of paper.

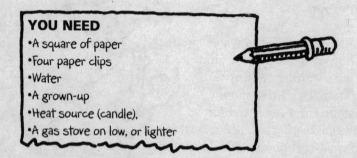

YOU NEED
- A square of paper
- Four paper clips
- Water
- A grown-up
- Heat source (candle),
- A gas stove on low, or lighter

SECRET PREPARATION
Crease the paper square as shown, then fold up the sides as in the last drawing, securing the corners with the paper clips.
This is your saucepan.

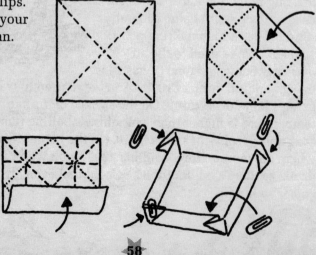

TO PERFORM

Inform your audience that in ancient Japan, houses were built of paper, in case they got knocked down by earthquakes. Paper saucepans were rarer, but they still worked.

There's no need to put too much water in the saucepan. The grown-up puts it over the heat, making sure that the flame only hits the middle of the bottom. Meanwhile you wave your arms and chant some mumbo jumbo. In a couple of minutes your astonished audience will see the water boil, but the saucepan remain untouched.

WHAT HAPPENED

Paper burns at 200°C. But your paper saucepan will stay at the same temperature as the water that soaks it, and the extraordinary thing is that the water will never get above 100°C, not never, no-how. As soon as any bit of water gets to 100°C (which is its boiling point), it boils, turns to steam, and floats up out of the saucepan. Boil as hard as you like for as long as you like, the paper won't burn until all the water has boiled away.

ICE PICK-UP

Although pure water boils at 100°C and freezes at 0°C, water with other things dissolved in it boils at higher temperatures and freezes at lower ones. We'll use that now in a bit more trickery.

THE EFFECT
Only the magician can pick up an ice cube without touching it.

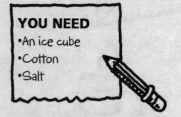

YOU NEED
• An ice cube
• Cotton
• Salt

TO PERFORM
Ask if anyone can work out how to pick up the ice cube using the cotton.

When they give up, lay the cotton over the top of the cube, sprinkle a tiny pinch of salt on it, and wait a minute. The ice will melt, then freeze again around the cotton. You can quite simply lift the cotton and the ice will come with it!

WHAT HAPPENED
The salt on the surface of the ice created a salt solution which has a lower freezing point than pure water, so the ice melted. Eventually, the water was able to freeze again, this time over the top of the cotton.

(Cooks add salt to the water of vegetables to raise the *boiling* point, so that the greens cook faster.)

CHAPTER FIVE

Bugs In Your Grub

For the next few magic tricks, we need the help of some assistants. Some very small assistants. So small, you can't see them. BUGS!

Bugs, germs, bacteria, microbes—call them what you will—there are an incredible number of these guys around. There are as many of them inside your kitchen as there are humans on the planet outside it. There are bugs on the table, squiggling across it with their tails thrashing; millions of bugs resting on the dish cloth, waiting to be wiped onto the oven when it's "cleaned." The drain is stuffed with them, and trillions more are floating through the air, hoping to land on something and set up home in your kitchen.

Can't see them though, can you? That's because they're so incredibly small. If you could get 100,000 of them to join hands in a line, they could ju-u-ust about stretch across this page.

But before you torch the whole place in disgust, remember that they are nearly all completely harmless. You are loaded with bugs, too, and they aren't doing you any harm at the moment, are they?

BUGS U LIKE!

In fact, a lot of bugs are vital. More than half your poo is bugs that live in your gut, doing magic tricks on your food. They feed on the food that floats past and pee chemicals which your body wants. The gut then sucks up these chemicals and thanks the bugs very much. It's a perfect relationship, even if it does sound utterly disgusting. The bugs get free meals and a nice warm, dark, damp home to bring up their children. The gut gets the vital chemicals your body needs to grow.

MAKE YOGURT MAKE YOGURT

In the fridge are foods which depend utterly on bugs doing magic transformations. When the yogurt pot says "live yogurt" on the side it means just that. There

are bugs inside it whose only ambition is to turn milk sour in a way that you find strangely tasty!

Get a grown-up to heat some milk until it's warm. Pour it into a bowl and mix in some live yogurt. Wrap it up and store it in a warm place. In less than a day, the whole bowl will have been turned to yogurt.

Another kind of bug turns milk sour in another way—a cheesy way. Yes, cheese could never happen without bugs. And how do you think those bubbles get into your bread? Yeast bugs!

MAKE YEAST MAKE BREAD

Mix up a cupful of warm sugary water, pour it into a bowl, stir in a teaspoonful of yeast, cover with a cloth, and keep it warm near a radiator. In an hour or so you will have a bowlful of brown froth.

The yeast bugs have had a feast on your sugar, enjoying themselves so much that they've farted a cloud of carbon dioxide bubbles. Bakers mix this with flour, bake it in the oven, and you enjoy the result. Bread is truly a work of fart.

GARDEN OF DISGUSTING DELIGHTS

Bugs may be too small for us to see them on their own, but when they make colonies of a million or so we can spot them.

A BUG GARDEN

THE EFFECT

The magician grows a **culture** of bugs big enough to see.

YOU NEED
- 2 teaspoons of agar (a kind of jelly you can get from the pharmacy)
- 1 teaspoon of sugar
- A cereal bowl
- Hot water (nearly boiling but not quite)

WHAT TO DO

Mix the agar and sugar together in a bowl filled to about 2 cm with hot water. Allow it to cool. You have just created a bug feast.

Now to collect some bugs. You could just leave the bowl out in the open; there are enough bugs in the air to populate it. But it's best to speed things up by wiping some tissue on a dirty spot in the house, then dipping that on to the agar, or just wiping it with a dishcloth, which is doubtlessly loaded with bugs.

Cover the bowl with plastic wrap and leave it somewhere out of the sun (sunshine kills bugs) and out of sight of grown-ups, who will have a fainting fit if they see what's going on.

Have a look after a week, if you can bear to. The dish will be covered with colored circles. Each one is a colony of bugs. The hairier circles are of fungus, which are a larger type of bug. The smoother circles are called bacteria (if you like them) or germs (if you don't).

Before you turn your nose up too far, remember that you are looking at your relations. Bacteria were the very first living things on the Earth. They appeared three thousand million years ago, and for two thousand million years they were the only life-form on the planet. Slowly they evolved into all the other plants and animals that have ever existed— including you!

VANISHING FOOD

There are huge nations of bugs in the soil of your garden. They can help you with the next magic miracle.

THE EFFECT
The magician makes a bag of food disappear.

YOU NEED
- Food waste chopped up small (use things like meal scraps, onion skins, lettuce stalks, and apple cores; don't use any hard things such as bones)
- A million assistants (you'll find them in the garden)

TO PERFORM
Choose your audience carefully. They must be very patient as this trick takes a fortnight. Tell them that you can make all those scraps of food disappear. Take them into the garden and bury them (the scraps, that is, not the audience).

Cover them with about 8 cm of soil and mark the spot. Tell the audience that this is very big magic and it will take you two weeks to complete the complex spell.

Of course, there isn't really any complex spell. What's actually happening is that the bugs in the soil are eating all the scraps and turning them into compost. However, if you come down to breakfast every morning deep in chants and magic gestures, the rest of your family might be impressed (or they might phone a doctor). The only thing you have to do is water the soil every two days.

In two weeks time take your audience to the same spot and ask them to hunt for the scraps. There will be no trace!

If you want more proof that the garden is full of bugs, have a sniff out there after it's been raining. That "earthy" smell so loved by poets is the combined smell of all their farts, squeezed out of the ground by the falling rain.

Bugs U Don't Like

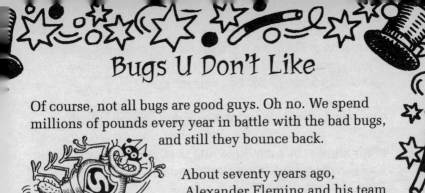

Of course, not all bugs are good guys. Oh no. We spend millions of pounds every year in battle with the bad bugs, and still they bounce back.

About seventy years ago, Alexander Fleming and his team of doctors were trying to beat the bad guys at their own game. The idea was to find a bug-eating bug that could do battle with the invaders. They were studying dishes of bugs exactly like that garden you made on page 65. One of the dishes had been attacked by a hasty fungus which had floated through a window, landed on the dish, and taken over; it squeezed out a juice that poisoned all the bacteria around. Fleming was about to throw the dish away in disgust, but then he stopped in his tracks. This was exactly what he wanted—something that would kill harmful bacteria! The fungus turned out to be from the very common penicillium family—the type that make lemons turn blue. So they named the new drug penicillin, and the rest is history. Ask your parents to think back a couple of generations—at least one of their relations would have died had it not been for penicillin.

The big problem with beating bugs is that you can blast away at them, swamp them with penicillin as much as you like, but if you don't quite finish the whole course of pills—if there is just one bug left . . . well, in ten minutes that one bug divides to make two, in another ten minutes those two make four, then eight, and from there the numbers increase at a truly mind-boggling rate.

Let's find out exactly how mind-boggling. You can use this in your next piece of magic.

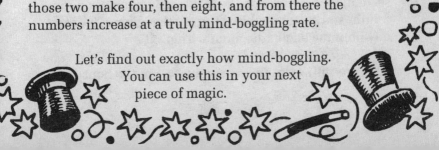

BECOME A POCKET
MONEY MILLIONAIRE

This shows the incredible rate at which things grow when they double over and over.

THE EFFECT

In just one month you become the richest person in the world.

YOU NEED

•Nothing but strong nerves

TO PERFORM

At the start of the month, search out the sources of pocket money. Tell them that at the end of this month you will never ask them for money ever again, ever.

Let this sink in. You'll know they have caught on when a strange smile appears on their face.

Tell them that in return they must agree to give you one penny on the first of the month, two pennies on the second, four pennies on the third, eight pennies on the fourth, and so on, doubling the number of pennies each day until the end of the month. That's it!

As a precaution, hide any calculators in the house, so

they can't work out what this actually means. As a second precaution get them to agree in writing, because they *will* work it out sooner or later, and then they definitely won't want to go through with it. How so? Find a calculator now and try it out. Punch in 0.01 (one penny is 0.01 of a dollar), then x2, x2, and so on thirty times. If you are smart enough to choose a month with thirty-one days in it, you should walk away with over twenty-one million dollars in all!

A BUG PROBLEM TO BUG YOU

This brain teaser is not as mathematical as it sounds, but it will annoy anyone you try it out on. Here goes . . .

Suppose a cockroach sits in a kitchen measuring 3 m x 3 m x 4 m. The cockroach takes up a volume of 3 mm x 3 mm x 3 mm. On day number 1 it produces a baby cockroach. They produce a baby each after another day, and so on. So each day, the population doubles.

If on day number 28 the kitchen is exactly full of cockroaches, on what day is the kitchen exactly half full of cockroaches?

Answer: If the room is exactly full on day 28, it is exactly half-full on day 27.

CHAPTER SIX

EGGSAMINATION: SEVEN EGGCITING AND EGGCENTRIC THINGS TO DO WITH EGGS

Let us eggstend your eggspertise by eggsploring some eggsotic eggsperiments with eggs. Eggsperience these eggstraordinary speggtacles.

CAN YOU TAKE THE SHELL OFF AN EGG WITHOUT BREAKING IT?

Put an egg in a jar of vinegar and leave it for about four days. On page 13 you found out that vinegar is an acid, quite good at "cutting" some substances. The acid will dissolve away the shell, but not the inner membrane and contents. It looks perfectly normal, but doesn't it feel weird?

CAN YOU EGGSPLAIN WHY BOILING EGGS BUBBLE?

On page 38 you saw how air expands when heated. Inside every egg there is a little sack of air. When the boiling water heats it up, the air expands and forces its way through tiny holes in the eggshell.

CAN YOU TOUCH THE EGG?

Put an egg in the middle of a wide glass full of rice. Now, can you touch it without touching the rice or tipping the glass?

Hold the glass as shown and firmly tap the top of the rim. Every time you tap, the contents shake around and some rice grains drop down below the egg, so it rides up slightly higher. The more you tap, the more it rises, until it breaks the surface. Then you can touch it easily.

CAN YOU TELL A RAW EGG FROM A BOILED ONE?

Spin two eggs, one raw and one boiled. The boiled one will spin merrily. But the liquid contents of the raw egg will tend to stay put when you spin the shell, so the raw egg will spin sluggishly.

CAN YOU MAKE AN EGG FLOAT IN WATER?

Whether an egg floats or not depends on the thickness (**density**) of the liquid it sits in. An egg won't float in ordinary tap water, but take it to the beach and float it in the sea (which is salty, and therefore thicker) and it will stay at the surface.

Or make some seawater yourself. Put an egg in warm water and it will sink. But pour salt in, stirring gently to help it dissolve, and the egg will magically rise to the surface.

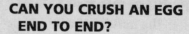

CAN YOU CRUSH AN EGG END TO END?

No, you can't! Eggs are famously frail, but try pushing them inward from the tips, and you'll be red and sweating before the egg shows any sign of distress. (We'll do some magic with this later.) If you try this, do it over a bowl, just in case something goes wrong!

CAN YOU HAVE YOUR EGG AND EAT IT?

Yes, you can! Next time you have a boiled egg, finish off eating it, then turn it over in the eggcup, clean the spoon, clear away the bits of eggshell and hand it back, saying you're not hungry after all.

CAN YOU BLOW AN EGG AWAY?

To do this you must empty an egg. Take a large needle and pierce the egg at either end. Wiggle the needle inside the egg to break up the yolk, then blow through one hole. The contents will come out of the other, leaving you with a hollow shell. Place this in an eggcup. Blow downward towards the rim of the eggcup and the egg will leap in the air.

CAN YOU MAKE AN EGG COMPLETELY DISAPPEAR?

Use the blown egg from the last magic trick. Leave it in a glass of vinegar for a few days, so the shell dissolves. All you have now is an egg-shaped membrane. It looks for all the world like a proper egg floating in the glass of vinegar, and provided nobody saw you, they'll be none the wiser. Tell them you are going to make it disappear.

Quickly pour the contents of the glass down the sink, but hold your fingers across the mouth of the glass while you do, catching the membrane and squashing it against the side of the glass. Everyone will be expecting to hear the egg scrunch into the sink. Allow them a quick glimpse of the apparently empty glass before inviting them to inspect the sink. As you turn towards the sink, remove and screw up the membrane. It's gone!

CHAPTER SEVEN
STRONG FOOD

This isn't a chapter on red-hot chili peppers. Food can be strong in other ways.

You've already seen how eggs show unexpected strength in certain directions because of their shape. Your local cathedral architect is well aware of this.

In fact, eggs are so strong that you can throw one 5 meters in the air and, so long as it lands on soft grass, it won't break.

We can use this strength for our own magic ends.

EGGSTRA STRENGTH

(I promise that's the last egg yolk!)

THE EFFECT
The magician makes a volunteer so light that they can stand on a packet of eggs.

YOU NEED
- A carton of six eggs
- Newspapers
- A piece of board, about foot-sized

TO PERFORM
Tell the audience that you will demonstrate the power of mind over matter. Choose a volunteer from among them (perhaps not the heaviest, just to be on the safe side).

Ask your volunteer, *"Do you think I've got beautiful eggs?"* Pause, while your volunteer tries to work out what you mean. Then say, *"I think I've got beautiful eggs, six of them, and here they are!"* Present the eggs. (Phew! They heard you wrong. You weren't talking about your legs after all.)

The power of mind over matter, you explain, involves the whole audience. By combining their minds in thought and focusing on the volunteer, they can make him or her light: so light that they can even stand on eggs without breaking them.

Prepare the eggs. Place a week's worth of papers nice and flat on the floor, place the carton of eggs on top, put another week's worth of papers on top, and the board on top of that.

These extras make sure that no single egg takes all the weight, but that it is spread evenly among all of them.

Holding the volunteer's hand, get them to place one foot carefully on the array, as much as possible at the center of the egg carton. Ask the audience to exercise their willpower and make the subject lighter . . . lighter . . . lighter. (The owner of the eggs will work particularly hard; they want their eggs back in one piece.)

Hold your volunteer's hand firmly while they transfer their weight from the foot on the floor to the foot on the carton. Get them to lift their back foot off the floor, so all the weight is on the carton. Let them hold it there for a beat, then—equally carefully—get them to step back down again. Display the undamaged eggs to the audience!

If the eggs break, this is your way out: tell them that this still demonstrated the power of mind over matter because you don't mind and they don't matter. Then run, before they throw the remains of the eggs after you.

SPAGHETTI TOWERS

Spaghetti is surprisingly strong if it's treated right. And when I say right, I mean upright. There's no trickery here, but you can make an hour magically fly by if you can find some spaghetti and some clay. Small pieces of clay hold the spaghetti ends while you build the strongest and tallest tower you can.

HELPFUL HINTS

1 You'll quickly find that the strongest structure is based on a triangular pyramid.

2 Put in cross-struts whenever you can.

3 Have several tries. You won't get the best structure on the first attempt. In the end, you should be able to build a tower 40–50 cm high.

SPUD U SPIKE

THE EFFECT
The magician gives a drinking straw amazing strength.

YOU NEED
- Drinking straws (if they have a crinkly section in the middle, cut them down—thin straws are the best)
- Potatoes

TO PERFORM
Ask the audience to try sticking a straw right through a potato. They will fail, of course.

Tell them, *"The power of concentration is one of my many skills. I will now concentrate all my energies on this straw to give it all my strength."*

Grip the straw firmly as shown and—most importantly— put your thumb over the end of the straw. Pause for a few seconds to build up the tension, then stab downward into the potato, fast, straight, and firmly. The straw will go right through.

WHAT HAPPENED
The essential ingredient of this trick is the thumb over the end of the straw. As the straw strikes the potato, the air inside it is forced upward. But it can't get out past the thumb, so it is compressed, it pushes outward, and the whole structure becomes rigid.

CAN DO, CAN DOES

This is similar to Eggstra Strength, but all you need is an empty soda can and a spoon, and there's a really snappy ending.

THE EFFECT
The heaviest person in the room is hypnotized by the magician. Suddenly they are as light as a feather.

TO PERFORM
As before, ask for a volunteer. This time, it doesn't matter how hefty—in fact, the bigger the better.

Place the can on the floor, near a table. Tell your volunteer that you are going to hypnotise them. You will make them very light. Swing the spoon in front of their face slowly, like a pendulum. Say, *"You are feeling sleepy ...very sleepy ... you are feeling lighter. Give me all your money ...that way you can lose pounds."*

Now ask them to put one foot on the can, then very carefully, using the table for support, stand on it, taking all their weight on that foot. The can will hold!

Then while they have all their weight there, tell them, *"When I tap my spoon, you will wake up and be your normal weight."* Bend down and tap the side of the can lightly. It will collapse, and your volunteer will wake up pretty rapidly!

WHAT HAPPENED

You can see there how strong a cylindrical structure can be if all the sides are straight, and how one slight dent at one point can weaken the whole thing, leading to a complete collapse.

In 1970, a rocket carrying three astronauts bound for the moon, *Apollo 13,* was nearly destroyed in midspace when an oxygen cylinder burst. During setup, the cylinder had been dropped, picking up a dent so small that nobody could see it. It was that dent which blew the cylinder and nearly killed the astronauts.

CHAPTER EIGHT
LEVERS

Of all the mechanical devices that crop up in the kitchen, the one that you'll find everywhere is the lever. There it is in all the handles, switches, can openers, bottle openers, etc., that you can find. Here's a trick that shows just how useful levers are.

✳ Magic ✳

RAISING A FAMILY

THE EFFECT
The smallest person in the neighborhood can lift up the largest.

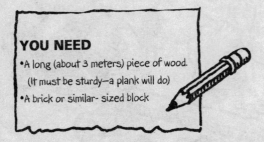

YOU NEED
• A long (about 3 meters) piece of wood. (It must be sturdy—a plank will do)
• A brick or similar- sized block

TO PERFORM
Ask the smallest person you can find (over the age of five) to step out in front. Ask for the biggest person there to step out as well. Ask the smallest person if they think they can lift up the biggest person. Ask the biggest person. Ask everyone. Nobody will believe it's possible.

Now get the smallest person to try. (If you have a wand, wave it like mad.) It won't do any good, of course. The largest person will remain stubbornly rooted to the floor.

Now introduce your magic plank—much bigger and much more effective than a poky old magic wand. Arrange it to pivot on the brick on the chair as shown, ask the largest person to sit on the short end, ask the smallest to pull down the long end, and witness the amazing power of the smallest, who can now lift the largest!

ARCHIMEDES,
KING OF THE LEVER

Although levers have been used for thousands of years, Archimedes was the person who first realized what incredible things could be done with them. He lived in Sicily, off the coast of Italy, two thousand years ago—so long ago that iron was a new-fangled gadget.

Archimedes' awesome inventions were mostly used in defense of his hometown, which was constantly being attacked by the bully boys of the Roman Empire. One of his most famous machines was a giant hook which would attach itself to an invading ship, then raise it bodily out of the water by means of a long lever. The mighty armies of Rome developed quite a respect for the little genius who stood between them and victory.

Archimedes reckoned there was no end to the uses a lever could be put to. His most famous remark was, "Give me somewhere to stand and I can move the Earth." He was perfectly correct, though he would have had to stand a long way away.

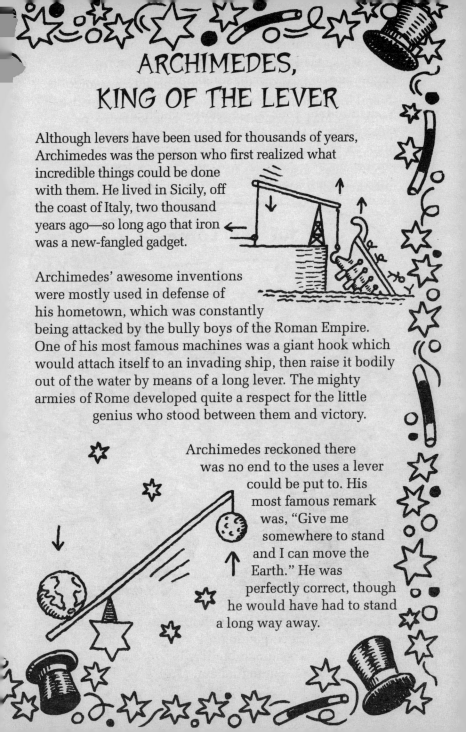

When the Roman armies eventually broke through Archimedes' defenses and captured his city, a soldier found him at home working on a mathematical treatise, bent over his papers. Instead of begging for mercy or surrendering, he merely said, "Don't disturb my diagrams." The soldier killed him on the spot. But Archimedes' discoveries have lived on after him. We use them all the time.

Hooray for the compound pulley!

One invention for which we should be eternally grateful was the compound pulley. If you don't know what a compound pulley is, you are about to find out. . . .

PULLEY PULLS THE PULLERS

THE EFFECT

The smallest person in the room has another task. This time, he or she is to be pitted against not one, but TWO of the biggest people around.

YOU NEED
- Two brooms or broom sticks
- About six meters of rope

TO PERFORM

When you have found your three assistants, tell them this is a tug of war: the two biggest against the one smallest. Ask them who is going to win. (Without doubt, they will get it wrong.)

Rig up the rope around the broom handles as shown.
Get the two biggest to hold the ends of the broom handles, so that the rope can slide easily over the sticks. All they have to do is to keep the brooms apart. Meanwhile the smallest takes the end of their rope and walks away with it. The arrangement of ropes ensures that in spite of all the efforts the two biggest make, they can't keep the brooms apart.
The smallest takes a bow!

WHAT HAPPENED

This is a crude version of Archimedes' compound pulley, a device which has been used in a hundred different countries in a thousand different ways, a million times a day, ever since Archimedes' death. The idea behind both the pulley and the lever is that you exchange a small movement with a lot of effort involved, for a big movement with only a little effort involved.

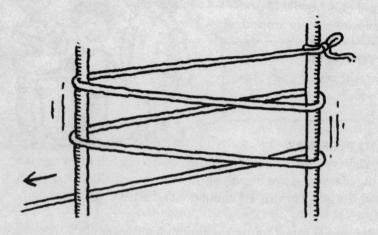

Long levers make hard jobs around the kitchen easy: cracking nuts, taking the tops off cans, etc. The opposite is also true: A small movement can be translated into a big one to make a little more magic. . . .

ELECTRIC MATCHES

THE EFFECT
The magician gives matches an electrostatic charge. When charged up, matches repel one another. To demonstrate, the magician holds one match near another, which shoots across the table. No one else can do the same thing.

YOU NEED
•Matches

SECRET PREPARATION
That stuff about electrostatic charges is total baloney. What you are really doing is flicking the matches with your fingers, so cleverly that nobody notices.

Here is how to hold the match. Grip it with your thumb and first finger almost at the bottom. (This is the pivot.) Hold it firmly. There should be a small piece of match still visible at the bottom. The second finger can push that down and let it flick back. That tiny movement of the finger on the short side of the match is translated into a huge flick at the long end.

This is the magician's-eye-view of the hand's position on the table (assuming you are right-handed). Notice that the match can only be flicked across the body. When you get it right, the flicking is completely invisible—the finger action at the bottom end is a tiny motion and the flick at the top is so fast nobody can follow it.

TO PERFORM

From here on it's all downhill. Say the right things and you can string the audience along forever. Tell your audience about electrostatic charges being like magnets. They can attract, like balloons sticking to a wall, or they can repel, like . . . well, like these matches! To "charge up" your match, rub it on your clothes, then it can "repel" the matches on the table.

When your audience fails to manage the same, try getting them to rub their matches on each other's clothes . . . on your clothes . . . perhaps they should hold the match a different way . . .

SEE YOUR OWN PULSE

There is a point on your wrist where you can feel your heartbeat. This is called your **pulse.** It's only a tiny movement, but using a bit of leverage you can see it clearly.

Stick a match on a push pin, as in the picture. Find the exact point on your wrist where the pulse is strongest and place the drawing pin there. The tip of the match will twitch visibly.

(To find your pulse, use three fingers in a row rather than your thumb. It's much quicker.)

MATCHLESS MATCH

If increasing the leverage makes us all superstrong, the opposite is also true. Without proper leverage we are all hopeless weaklings. Could you open a door if the handle was down by the hinge? Could you flush the toilet if there was no lever? Could you break a match? Not if you hold it like this . . .

SIT-UP-AND-BEG BOX

Many magic tricks rely on the hidden power of levers. This one is simple, but dramatic.

THE EFFECT
The magician makes a matchbox stand up when commanded.

YOU NEED
- A matchbox
- A hanky

SECRET PREPARATION
Use a match to help you wedge a tiny piece of the hanky between the bottom of the drawer and the outer case, as in the picture. Provided the hanky is not too smooth and neat, this minuscule tuck will not be noticeable.

TO PERFORM
Place the hanky and matchbox on the table with the box lying across you. Hold the hanky on either side.

Now try to get the matchbox to stand up. It is important to fail for a long time—this builds up the suspense. Say, "*Sit up boy ... beg ...okay, play dead.*"

It is the last command which works. Simply pull outward on the hanky. The tiny movement of the hanky is enough to push the box upright.

CHAPTER NINE
BIG STOMACH MAGIC

We started with bicarb. We talked about heat. We discused strong structures. Let's combine them all together and eat the result.

HONEYCOMB

YOU NEED
- 200 grams sugar
- A quarter of a pint of water
- A saucepan
- A heaped teaspoon bicarb
- A stove
- A grown-up

WHAT TO DO
Get the grown-up to pour the sugar and water into the saucepan and heat up, stirring constantly. The sugar will dissolve as the agitated water molecules rip into the sugar grains and tear them apart. The water will evaporate slowly, but the sugar will remain, because it's got a higher boiling point. So the solution will thicken up.

Meanwhile, dissolve the bicarb in a little water and wait for the right moment.

When the sugar solution is beginning to turn brown (turning into a toffee color), take the saucepan off the stove and quickly mix in the bicarb, stirring vigorously. The sugar will foam up.

Pour the mixture onto a greased plate and allow to cool. The result is light, strong, and very nice to eat.

Answer to The Obedient Raisin mystery:

The raisin rises when bubbles form on it. The bubbles float up to the surface, dragging the raisin with them, but at the top they burst. The raisin is now heavier than water and sinks to the bottom again, where more bubbles form on it, which . . . and so on until there's no fizz left in the drink.

LIST OF MAGIC TRICKS

You have mastered the magic of your kitchen, now try this trick from *Science Magic in the Bathroom:*

THE NO-SPILL SPELL

L et's see just how strong the skin on water really is.

THE EFFECT
Water rises above the top of a glass with no visible means of support, held up by the psychic powers of the magician.

YOU NEED
- A glass of water
- A pile of coins
- A tray to perform the trick in
  (There may be some spilling)

TO PERFORM
Ask an assistant to fill the glass right up to the brim. Make sure that the water is absolutely level with the top.

Now you must both concentrate on the water, and persuade it to rise higher. Is it persuaded? Try dropping a coin in very carefully. Then a few more. Keep going, dropping in the coins ever so carefully until the water rises over the top of the glass. Have a look at how many coins the glass took. That's powerful persuasion!

WHAT HAPPENED?
The surface tension held the water in the glass. If you look very closely you can see the meniscus clinging to the edge of the glass and bowing upwards and over the top.

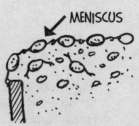

MENISCUS